The Best Responses to Overcome Sales Objections

Pocket-Guide

by

Billy R. Williams, Ph.D.

Table of Contents

Introduction

This easy-to-use pocket-guide will equip you with effective responses that help turn objections into opportunities.

Sales can be a challenging journey, and objections are a natural part of it.

However, armed with the right responses and strategies outlined in this pocket-guide, you'll be well-prepared to navigate objections seamlessly, manage emotions effectively, and steer conversations toward successful outcomes.

To help keep this pocket-guide as an easy-to-use resource, I will not give you comprehensive training on Triggers, Workflows, Sales Funnels, Autoresponders, and other tools and automation that can and should be a part of your business.

Instead, this pocket-guide will focus on the situation and the various responses you can use within that situation.

For a detailed and comprehensive look at triggers, workflows, automation, etc., check out my book "Inbound Marketing 101. How 2 Make Your Business a Magnet for Inbound Prospects"

https://www.amazon.com/Inbound-Marketing-Business-Magnet-Prospects/dp/1533547866

The Best Responses to Overcome Sales Objections - Pocket-Guide" is a small and handy book made for salespeople from any industry.

It gives quick and great ways to handle objections during the 5 main areas of the sales cycle where you will most likely face objections:

1. When initially contacting your lead or prospect

2. When you must leave a voicemail

3. When trying to gather information from your lead or prospect

4. When trying to follow-up with your lead or prospect

5. When closing the sale.

The best salespeople in the world always have a response regardless of the situation.

The responses we provide in this Best Responses Pocket-Guide will help you not only manage a lead, prospect, or customer's emotions, it will also help you manage your emotions, which is the most essential step in overcoming sales objections.

Why you should listen to Dr. Billy R. Williams

In the Army, I was a Station Commander in charge of Army College Recruiting. I was a 2-time recruiter of the year. In the civilian world, I started as a captive insurance agent for Allstate. During my time with Allstate, I won many awards and accolades including the Star Performer Award, and the prestigious Century Club Award for writing 100 new items per month for 12 straight months.

I left Allstate and started the Williams Family Investment and Insurance Group (WFIG). WFIG has grown to a group of 150 plus partner insurance agencies that in total write over a billion dollars in new and renewal insurance premiums each year.

That is not me bragging, but simply laying the foundation to help you understand why I have the experience and credibility to write a Pocket Guide on Overcoming Sales Objections.

I have trained and mentored 1000's of salespeople and I can quickly tell the good ones from the bad ones. How do you ask? because the good ones understand how to control the emotion of the situation by asking the right questions, having the right responses, and not letting the prospect's or customer's emotions control how the salesperson goes about their job.

Because this is a pocket-guide I will save most of the details and explanations that help you understand the thought process behind the scripts and templates for the final sections of the pocket-guide.

Using this Best Responses Pocket-Guide is very simple:

1. Identify the situation,

2. Select the type of communication method(s) you want to use,

3. Locate the recommended responses based on the situation in the pocket guide,

4. Select the script or template from the pocket-guide that you believe will be the most effective, and

5. Use our recommended response(s) in their exact form or use them as a foundation and modify them to your personality when communicating with your lead, prospect, or customer.

Enough talk. Let's get started!

Chapter One: The Basics of the Best Responses to Overcome Sales Objections

In this Pocket Guide I will give you responses that you can quickly access and use in the 5 main areas of the sales cycle where you will most likely face objections:

1. When initially contacting your lead or prospect

2. When you must leave a voicemail

3. When trying to gather information from your lead or prospect

4. When trying to follow-up with your lead or prospect

5. When closing the sale.

Tools you will need to maximize your responses to sales objections.

1. A Business Card (Paper and/or Digital)

2. An Introduction Video

3. A Phone (Mobile, Soft Phone, or Land Line)

4. An Email Program (Preferably with Merge Field Capabilities)

5. A Text Message Tool (Phone or Online)

6. Social Networking Profile (Business and/or Personal)

7. Video Recording Tool (Examples: Loom or Snagit)

8. Appointment Scheduling Tool (Examples: Calendly or Bookings)

9. Phone Call Scripts

10. Voicemail Scripts

11. Email Templates

12. Text Message Templates

13. Social Networking Direct Message Templates

14. (Optional) Customer Relationship Manager (CRM)

Special CRM Note:

The Inspire a Nation Data Super Center CRM contains all the templates discussed in this pocket guide as well as easy to implement sales funnels, autoresponders, and automated workflows. Start all of your Best Response templates, emails, and text messages with one click of a button.

See more details at https://www.inspireanation.org/Data-Super-Center/

The 3-Step Objection Response Process that will turn Objections into Opportunities:

1. Allow the lead or prospect to give you their objection,

2. Give a response (Use the Pocket-Guide to select the best response)

3. Give your Elevator Pitch.

The Goal of a Good Response is to:

1. Get the prospect's permission to continue talking,

2. Give your elevator speech (Features + Benefits + Consequences),

3. Gather data you need to offer your product or service,

4. Schedule an appointment if you can't gather data right now, or

5. Get a priority contact date so you know when the conversation will be important to the prospect. (The date the product or service ends, runs out, is needed again, and the contact's birthday!)

What is an Elevator Speech?

An elevator speech has 4 components: Features + Benefits + Consequences + Permission to keep talking.

- Features = A feature is how a product or service works, its function, or its purpose

- Benefit = How a product or service makes your life better, easier, more fun, etc.

- Consequence = What happens at the moment you need a product or service, and you don't have it.

- Permission to Keep Talking = When you ask the customer if they will agree to listen to the next thing you want to say. (Example: "It takes about 90 seconds for me to explain it, can I talk for 90 more seconds?")

Insurance Elevator Speech Example:

"Insurance provides 3 buckets of money when you file a claim, money that is paid directly to you and your family, money that is paid to others on your behalf, and money that is paid to repair or replace the things you have insured. Without the right insurance when you have a claim, you could end up spending thousands of dollars out of pocket instead of spending a few dollars on month to have the right insurance. I don't know your individual situation, but if you tell me a couple of quick facts, I can give you my professional insight, and if we need to delve deeper, we can schedule an appointment."

To make it easy to use the pocket-guide I will provide templates and scripts you will need to respond to sales objections, including:

1. Conversation Script (P = Phone)

2. Voicemail Template (V – Voicemail)

3. Email Template (E = Email)

4. Text Message Template (T = Text Message)

5. Social Networking Direct Message Template (S = Social Networking DM)

6. Personalized Video Script (V = Personalized Video)

7. Face-to-Face (F = Face-to-Face Script)

To make it easy for you to understand the best responses, often I will use names and not just place holders so that you can get a better feel for the conversation.

Chapter Two: Responses to common Objections

Responses to objections can take on different complexities and formats depending on where in the sales cycle you encountered the objection. Some responses can be simple one or two sentence responses, and some will require more detailed talking points.

I am going to give you two different levels of responses: Simple and advanced. Each level increases in dialogue and tries to achieve more of the five goals of a good response.

As a quick reminder, the Goal of a Good Response is to:

1. Get the prospect's permission to continue talking,

2. Give your elevator speech (Features + Benefits + Consequences),

3. Gather data you need to offer your product or service,

4. Schedule an appointment if you can't gather data right now, or

5. Get a priority contact date so you know when the conversation will be important to the prospect. (The date the product or service ends, runs out, is needed again, and the contact's birthday!)

Objection: It is too expensive!

Objection: It's too expensive (Simple Responses)

It's Too Expensive (Simple Response 1): "Even though it seems too expensive upfront, it will save you money in the long run. Let me show you what I mean. It will take me a few minutes to show you what I mean. Do you have a few minutes right now? "

It's Too Expensive (Simple Response 2): "We will look at different payment options until we find something that still gets you what you want but works with your budget. I need to ask some questions; do you have some time right now?"

It's Too Expensive (Simple Response 3): " Let's me know what you can afford, and I will work to find something that fits that number. If you will work with me, we can figure this out. Are you ready to get started?"

It's Too Expensive (Simple Response 4): "I understand that money is tight right now. Let's look at removing some of the more advanced features and benefits and see if we can find something that fits in your budget. I need to ask a few more questions. The first question is . . . ?"

It's Too Expensive (Simple Response 5): "Let's look at dropping down a level or two and see if we can find something that works with your budget. I need you to tell me what you want to get rid of and what you want to keep. Can we do that now?

It's Too Expensive (Simple Response 6): "What budget are we working with? I can't promise I can fit your budget, but I will do my best. Give me a few more minutes and I will see what I can work out."

It's Too Expensive (Simple Response 7): "Let me see if there are discounts or incentives that are available that could reduce the price. I need to do a little more digging. Do you have time right now to see if I can find you some discounts?"

It's Too Expensive (Simple Response 8): "No problem. We can start with a lower priced option, and then as your budget improves, we can move up to the options that are best for you. Let's take a few minutes to see where we should start."

It's Too Expensive (Simple Response 9): "Give me a few more minutes and I can show you how our (product or service) makes it a good investment, despite the initial cost. Can I have your permission to show you what I mean?

It's Too Expensive (Simple Response 10): If you can't afford the full package right now, we can phase in parts of the package over time until we get you where you want to be. Let me ask a few more questions so I am sure we are starting at the right place."

Objection: It's too expensive (Advanced Responses)

In the following advanced response scenarios, I am going to use the response format:

"The purpose of the (product or service) is to make sure that a (consequence) doesn't impact your quality of life. I need more information to better understand what is going on."

It's Too Expensive (Advanced Response 1): "I understand you're concerned about the price. Let me explain why it's worth the cost and offer you payment options to make it more affordable. Because I want to make sure you fully understand what I am working out for you, do me a favor and grab something to take notes while we work this out."

It's Too Expensive (Advanced Response 2): "If you don't have all the money you need to get this started today, I have several financing options we can explore. You might have to give up buying a coffee or eating out once a week, but the peace of mind you will have will be more than worth it. This is going to take a few more minutes. Do you have time right now or should we schedule a different time to finish this?"

It's Too Expensive (Advanced Response 3): "Many people only look at the final number without looking at how this purchase will improve their overall quality of life. Put the numbers out of your head for a second and let's look at how it impacts your quality of life. If that causes the final price to make more sense, we can move on, if not, we can look at other options."

It's Too Expensive (Advanced Response 4): "While I want you to have all of the features and benefits of this (product or service), reality is, if you can't afford this level, we will have to drop down a level or two and get you the maximum we can at the budget you have to work with. Let's do some more work and find what you can afford. Do you have the time right now to finish this?"

It's Too Expensive (Advanced Response 5): My goal is to give you the maximum features and benefits that I can while staying within your budget. I will need to do some more digging and ask more questions to see where features, benefits, and budget all come together. Do you have time right now, or should we schedule a different time that works better for you?

It's Too Expensive (Advanced Response 6): (Insurance Example)

"Insurance provides 3 buckets of money when you file a claim, money that is paid directly to you and your family, money that is paid to others on your behalf, and money that is paid to repair or replace the things you have insured. Without the right insurance when you have a claim, you could end up spending thousands of dollars out of pocket instead of spending a few dollars each month to have the right insurance. I don't know your individual situation, but if you tell me a couple of quick facts, I can give you my professional insight. Do you have time to have a quick discussion with me right now, or should we find a time that works better for both of us?

It's Too Expensive (Advanced Response 7): (Roofing Example)

You always want the damage to your roof repaired as quickly as possible. Because you rarely go into your attic, you might not notice a small leak in your roof. A small leak can cause a lot of damage over time. I don't know if you have damage, but if you will let me take a quick look at your roof, I can let you know what is going on up there. I will have my inspectors in your area Tuesday and Wednesday. Which day works best for you?

It's Too Expensive (Advanced Response 8): (Carpet Cleaner Example)

Dirty carpets don't just look bad, they also trap allergens, dead bugs, and other pretty nasty stuff. Clean carpets can save people from spending more money on air-fresheners and allergy medicines than they do on getting their carpets cleaned. I have a quick test that shows you what a clean section of your carpet looks like compared to a dirty section. It will take me about 5 minutes to show you what I mean. Do you have 5 minutes right now, or should we schedule a time later this week?

It's Too Expensive (Advanced Response 9): (Hairstylist Example)

My product or service is designed to keep your hair healthy and created to keep you from having problems with your hair such as breakage, split ends, and thinning. I always get the too expensive response before someone has a problem with their hair, but when they actually have a problem, they will gladly pay me two or three times the original price to fix the problem. I can't spend your money for you, but I can give you my professional insight. The only way I can determine what is going on with your hair is for me to look at it. Hair assessment appointments are $10.00 and take about 10 minutes. If you are interested, I can send you a link to my appointment calendar where you can book and pay for the assessment online. Do you want the link sent by email, text message, or both?

Objection: I'm not interested in your product or service!

Objection: "I'm not interested in your product or service. (Advanced Responses Only. There are no simple responses to this objection!)

Not Interested - Response 1: "No problem. I don't expect you to be interested yet because I haven't shown you anything that makes your life better. Give me 60 seconds to give you my pitch and if you are still not interested, I won't waste any more of your time. Is that easy enough? (Start your elevator pitch with consequences, not benefits) (See Not Interested – Advanced (Insurance Example))

Not Interested –Response 2: "So I can update my notes, are you not interested because it is not a priority to get this taken care of right now, or it is not important to you at all? If now is not a priority, I will contact you when it becomes more of a priority. When do you anticipate it becoming a priority?

Not Interested –Response 3: If I can show you how our product or service can make your life better and easier, and possibly save you some money, would that be of interest to you? Give me 60 seconds to explain what we do, and if you are still not interested, I won't take up any more of your time. Can I have 60 seconds of your time?

Not Interested –Response 4: "I get that a lot because people assume I will only waste their time and not improve their quality of life in any way, but once they give me 60 seconds and hear what I have to say, many of them are glad they didn't just hang up on me (or walk away). Will you give me 60 seconds so I can see if we can make a difference in your quality of life?

Not Interested – Response 5: "Is there something specific that you are not interested in? Was there a specific need that you wanted to address that I didn't give enough attention to? If you felt we rushed through this, let's schedule an additional time so we can slow things down and really delve deeper into this. Do you want to meet by phone, video meeting, or in-person?"

Not Interested – Response 6: "Often, it's a timing issue. Did I reach you at a time that my product or service is not a priority right now? Let's meet when my product or service is more of a priority?" Do you want to meet by phone, video meeting, or in-person?"

Not Interested – Response 7: "Thanks for letting me know. If anything changes or if you have questions later, I'm going to leave you my contact information. Do you want me to get that to you by email, text message, or both? I am also going to include a short video and a link to our Google Review page so you can see what others are saying about our business. I want to be your first thought when you need what we offer.

Not Interested – Advanced Response 8: "Are you not interested at all, or do you have more important things to take care of right now and you don't want to get pulled off your agenda? Take care of what you need to take care of, and let's find a time to meet when this is more of a priority for you. Do you want to schedule something right now, or do you want me to text you my appointment calendar, so you can choose a day and time that works better for you?"

Not Interested – Advanced Response 9: "Most people are not interested until they hear about our deep discounts and the special promotions that we have going on right now. Give me 30 seconds and I can show you what I am talking about."

Not Interested – Advanced Response 10: "No worries. I don't expect you to be interested until I make it interesting to you and show you how our products and services can make your life easier. All I need is 60 seconds of your time and your permission to keep talking. Will you give me that permission?

Not Interested – Advanced Response 11: "I know your time is valuable so I recorded a short video, that you can watch at any time, that explains how our products and services can potentially make your life better and easier. How do you want me to get that over to you by email, text message, or both?"

Objection: "I'm not interested in your product or service." (Advanced Responses)

Not Interested - Advanced Response 12: "I wouldn't expect you to be interested just yet, since I haven't shown you any value or benefit that would change your current situation. But 90 seconds from now if you are still not interested that means I didn't do a good job, so do me a favor and give me a grade 90 seconds from now so I can improve my conversation and show value sooner. Will you do that for me? Great!"

Not Interested – Advanced Response 13 (Insurance Example): "The moment someone files a claim and realizes they will have to pay $1000's of dollars out of pocket to get their items repaired because their insurance was cheap, but not good, is when they remember this conversation, and contact me to see how I can help them, unfortunately by then it is too late, and because of the claim, often, I can't move them to good insurance so they are trapped paying two or three times what they would have paid if they had made the right decision up front. I don't know if you have the right insurance for your unique situation, but if you let me do a little fact finding, I can give you my professional assessment. Do you have time right now, or should we schedule at a time that works best for both of us?"

Not Interested – Advanced Response 14: "[First Name], you always want a competitor to give you a second opinion because we will point out any weaknesses or problems we find since we want to compete for your business. I want to be the competitor that sharpshoots your current situation and discovers the weaknesses or validates you have the best coverage. Will you give me a few minutes to do that for you? DELIVER YOUR PITCH! What grade did I earn? What did I miss that was important to you?

Objection: I don't Have Time to Talk Right Now

I don't have time to talk right now (Simple Responses)

I don't have time to talk right now (Simple Response 1): "I understand, and I want to be respectful of your time. It will take me 90 seconds to show you how my product or service can improve your situation. Can I have 90 seconds of your time?"

I don't have time to talk right now (Simple Response 2): "I completely respect that. Can I quickly summarize the main benefits in a video and email and text it to you to review when you have a moment?"

I don't have time to talk right now (Simple Response 3): "We can split our conversation into 10- or 15-minute blocks of time. It will mean we have to have multiple conversations, but it also means you don't have to give me a big block of your time in one sitting.

I don't have time to talk right now (Simple Response 4): "I know your time is valuable. Can I quickly highlight the key benefits, and if it piques your interest, we can arrange a more detailed discussion for later?"

I don't have time to talk right now (Simple Response 5): "I'm here to make the process go as easy as possible. Would 5 minutes now be manageable for a quick conversation?"

I don't have time to talk right now (Simple Response 6): No problem. I can summarize everything in two minutes and any questions you have after that, we can schedule a follow-up meeting to address.

I don't have time to talk right now (Simple Response 7): I know this is important to you, so let's schedule a follow-up meeting so that solving this issue is not just important, but also a priority. I have my calendar open, does Tuesday or Wednesday morning work best for you?

I don't have time to talk right now (Advanced Responses)

I don't have time to talk right now (Advanced Response 1): I try to make it as easy as possible to do business with me, so here is what I can do, let's schedule an appointment now so we will have a guaranteed date on the calendar, and we can continue to talk for a few minutes until you run out of time and have to go. That should give me enough information to start working on your plan/quote.

I don't have time to talk right now (Advanced Response 2): I anticipated you would say that, so I created a short video that explains most of the important things you need to know. I will text it over to you. The video gives me a timestamp when you open it and that lets me know you have had a chance to watch the video prior to our next meeting. It also has a button on the top right of the video that allows you to schedule a time on my appointment calendar to finish our conversation.

I don't have time to talk right now (Advanced Response 3): I know taking care of this situation is important, but is it actually a priority right now? If it is not a priority, I'm going to keep reaching out and you are going to keep avoiding me, and it becomes uncomfortable for both of us. Let's schedule a meeting closer to the time this issue becomes more of a priority to take care of. When do you see this becoming a priority?

I don't have time to talk right now (Advanced Response 4 – Insurance Example): I respect your time, and I am sure as another professional you respect mine as well. Is this something that will eventually become a priority as you get closer to your upcoming insurance renewal date? When does your current insurance expire? I don't want to add to your workload when it is not a priority, so I am going to build a date to follow-up with you in my calendar and send you a confirmation and reminder a few days prior to me reaching out. This way we can talk when it is important and a priority for both of us. Is Tuesday, Wednesday, or Thursday usually better for you?

I want to shop around some more.

1. "Of course! It's always a good idea to explore options. What specific features are you interested in comparing?"

2. "I completely understand. When you're ready, I'd be happy to assist you in comparing our features with other options."

3. "Thank you for considering your options. Is there anything specific you're looking for in a product that I can provide more information about?"

4. "Great! Evaluating multiple options is a smart approach. If you need any assistance with comparisons or have questions, feel free to reach out."

5. "No problem at all. I'd suggest looking at factors like features, pricing, and customer support in your comparison. Let me know if you need more details on our offerings."

6. "Absolutely, it's important to make an informed decision. What aspects of our product would you like to compare with our competitors?"

7. "Thank you for being thorough in your research. Is there any information you need from me to aid in your comparison?"

8. "I appreciate your diligence in exploring options. Is there a particular timeline you have in mind for making a decision?"

9. "Certainly! If you have any questions or need assistance while comparing, I'm here to help."

10. "I understand. When you're ready, we can discuss how our product stands out in comparison to others."

11. "Thank you for your honesty. Is there a specific aspect of our product you'd like more information on to aid in your comparison?"

12. "No worries! Take your time to explore. Is there a specific criterion you're looking for in a product that I can address?"

13. "I appreciate your thoroughness. If there's anything you'd like to know about our product during your comparison, please feel free to ask."

14. "Absolutely, exploring options is a wise approach. What specific benefits are you hoping to find in a product?"

15. "Thank you for considering your choices carefully. When you're ready, I'd be happy to walk you through what sets our product apart."

16. "Noted. Is there any particular information you'd like from us to facilitate your comparison with other products?"

17. "I understand your need to research. If there's any additional information you need, don't hesitate to ask."

18. "Of course! It's essential to have a clear understanding of your options. Is there a deadline you're working towards for making a decision?"

19. "Thank you for your honesty. What criteria are most important to you when evaluating products?"

20. "I respect your decision to explore. Is there a specific area where you'd like to focus your comparison?"

21. "No problem at all. I'd recommend considering factors like reliability, features, and support while comparing. Let me know if you need assistance with any of those."

22. "Thank you for considering your choices thoughtfully. Is there anything specific you'd like to know about our product as you compare options?"

23. "Absolutely, comparing helps you make an informed choice. If you need additional information or have questions, I'm here to assist."

24. "I appreciate your thorough approach. Is there any particular information you're seeking during your comparison process?"

25. "Understood. When you're ready, let's discuss how our product aligns with your needs and goals."

We've been working with our current vendor for years, and we're loyal to them."

1. "I respect loyalty to your current vendor. Let's discuss how we can complement what you already have."

2. "Loyalty is admirable. Can you share what specific aspects of their service have kept you with them?"

3. "It's great that you have a strong relationship with your current vendor. What would it take for you to consider adding us as a backup or alternative?"

4. "We're not asking you to switch right away. How about giving us a chance to show you what we can offer alongside your current vendor?"

5. "Loyalty is valuable. Exploring options doesn't mean you have to abandon your current vendor. It's about having choices."

6. "That loyalty speaks highly of your values. How about a no-obligation trial to see how we can enhance your current setup?"

7. "Maintaining good relationships is important. We can work with your vendor or even integrate our solutions to complement their services."

8. "Loyalty is commendable. What if we can provide a unique service that could work alongside your current vendor?"

9. "I understand the loyalty you have. Let's discuss ways our services might add value without disrupting your current setup."

10. "Loyalty is key, and we appreciate that. How about a side-by-side comparison to see where we shine?"

11. "I get it, loyalty is a strong bond. What specific challenges or improvements would make you consider exploring other options?"

12. "Your loyalty to your vendor is impressive. Let's talk about where we excel and see if there's a good fit."

13. "Loyalty is something to be proud of. We can work with your vendor to provide additional benefits you might not have considered."

14. "Loyalty is a great foundation. Would you be open to a discussion about how our services can complement what you already have?"

15. "Your loyalty speaks volumes. Let's see if we can find ways to enhance your current setup with our solutions."

16. "We're not here to replace, but to enhance. How about exploring the ways we can work alongside your current vendor?"

17. "Your loyalty is admirable. Let's consider how we can provide a safety net or a backup solution for your peace of mind."

18. "Loyalty is important, and we respect that. What if we can address specific pain points or gaps you've experienced with your current vendor?"

19. "We're not asking you to break ties. Let's explore how we can support your current relationship and provide added value."

20. "Loyalty should be celebrated. What are the pain points you'd like to see addressed with your current vendor?"

21. "Your loyalty is important. How about a low-risk trial to see how we can complement what you're already getting?"

22. "It's great to hear about your loyalty. We're here to offer you an alternative or support where needed."

23. "Loyalty is a strength, and we want to respect that. Let's explore how we can collaborate with your current vendor."

24. "We're not here to disrupt your loyalty. Let's talk about how we can fill in any gaps or offer you an extra layer of support."

25. "Loyalty is something we admire. How can we tailor our services to enhance your existing partnership?"

I need to talk to someone else before I can decide.

1. "No worries, it's usually a team effort. Who else is weighing in on this?"

2. "That's cool. Who else is in on this decision-making party?"

3. "Sure thing! What are they gonna want to know?"

4. "Got it. How do you see the gang tackling this?"

5. "Team discussions? Nice! How long before they huddle up?"

6. "Thanks for the heads-up. Any tips from past discussions on how to make it smooth sailing?"

7. "As you chat with your crew, what can we do to make it a breeze?"

8. "Perfect! What's on their minds as you chat with the gang?"

9. "Sounds good. Let's arm you with the info you need to pitch our solution like a pro."

10. "Teamwork makes the dream work, right? How can we help as you huddle with your crew?"

11. "What do you think will be the hot topics during your chat with the gang?"

12. "I've been down this road before. How can we make it smooth as butter for you?"

13. "Expecting any curveballs or concerns during the team chat? Let's prep for those."

14. "Team decisions rock! Let's make sure everyone's got the scoop for a productive chat."

15. "Who's the real MVP in these team decisions? What are their main interests?"

16. "Can you give me the lowdown on the key players? It'll help us get ready."

17. "We're here to back you up. What's your plan for making this chat a hit?"

18. "We're all ears. How can we support the discussion and help everyone see eye to eye?"

19. "How about we catch up again after the team talk? What works for you?"

20. "Teamwork for the win! What's next in your game plan?"

21. "In group chats, making sure everyone's heard is key. What's your play for that?"

22. "Any burning questions from your team we should address?"

23. "Let's ensure everyone's on the same page. Anything else you want to dig into?"

24. "Team chats can be a game-changer. How can we help make it a slam dunk for you?"

25. "Team chats are all about synergy. How can we make the process smoother than a fresh jar of peanut butter?"

I need more time to think about it. Can you follow up with me in a few months?

1. "No worries! Take your time. What's on your mind that you want to think about?"

2. "Sure thing! What's the most important stuff you want to weigh during this time?"

3. "Absolutely, I get it. What's the big picture for you in the next few months?"

4. "No rush. What changes or decisions are you expecting in the coming months?"

5. "Taking your time is cool. What kind of info or help do you need while you're thinking?"

6. "I understand. What issues or challenges do you think might pop up in this period?"

7. "Sure, we can follow up. What's the best way for us to keep you updated?"

8. "No problem. What can we do to support you while you're making your decision?"

9. "Absolutely, we can reconnect later. What questions or updates are you looking for in the meantime?"

10. "Taking it slow, I like that. What should we focus on in our follow-up conversation?"

11. "I respect your pace. How can we assist you during this time?"

12. "I get it. How can we keep you in the loop in the next few months?"

13. "Sure, no pressure. What kind of help or info would be most useful to you during this period?"

14. "No rush at all. What information do you want to ensure you have while you're thinking?"

15. "I appreciate your patience. What can we do to meet your needs during this time?"

16. "Taking your time is a good call. What goals are you aiming for before making a decision?"

17. "We can definitely follow up. What's on your mind that you'd like to explore?"

18. "I completely respect your decision. How can we make sure our next chat is helpful for you?"

19. "No problem, we can reconnect later. What do you want to learn or understand better in the meantime?"

20. "Your need for time is clear. How can we stay connected and assist you over the next few months?"

21. "Taking your time is a smart choice. How can we back you up in your decision-making process?"

22. "I respect your choice. What specific things would you like to see happen during this period?"

23. "Absolutely, we can follow up. What aspects are most important for you to look at?"

24. "No problem, we'll chat later. What's the big focus for you during this time?"

25. "I appreciate your need for time. How can we make sure our next conversation is spot-on for you?"

We're too busy with other projects, and we don't have the time to focus on implementing a new solution.

1. "I totally get it, you've got a lot on your plate. Let's see if our solution can make your life easier, not busier."

2. "Busy is good! What if our solution could help you get more done with less effort?"

3. "No worries, we can make this easy. Our solution won't add extra work; it's all about simplifying things."

4. "I know time is tight. We'll handle the heavy lifting, so you can stay focused on what you do best."

5. "I understand, it's project galore. We can work around your schedule to make things smooth."

6. "Busy times are common. Let's consider an easy-to-adopt solution that won't disrupt your flow."

7. "I respect that your time is valuable. Our solution can be tailored to fit seamlessly into your day."

8. "Time matters, and we won't waste it. Let's keep things hassle-free and aligned with your workflow."

9. "Your time is precious, and we're here to make it count. Let's see how our solution can be a game-changer."

10. "Busy or not, we're here to make your life easier. We'll handle the hard stuff for you."

11. "Your projects are important. We can make this transition a breeze so you can keep focusing on what matters."

12. "No problem, we'll work around your schedule. Let's make this a piece of cake."

13. "Time is money, and we don't want to break the bank. Our solution is user-friendly and quick to set up."

14. "We respect your busy schedule. Let's talk about how our solution can be your secret productivity weapon."

15. "We're here to save you time, not eat it up. How about we chat about how we can make your day smoother?"

16. "Success keeps you busy, and we want to be part of that journey. Our solution is designed to enhance, not complicate, your projects."

17. "I get it; you don't have time to waste. Let's discuss a plan that respects your time and gets you results fast."

18. "Your time is valuable, and we'll make the most of it. Let's keep it simple and effective."

19. "Don't worry about being busy; we'll fit right in. Let's explore how our solution can work with your schedule."

20. "Busy times are part of the game. We can be flexible and make things work without adding stress."

21. "I appreciate your honesty about your workload. Our solution is designed to be a time-saver, not a time-drain."

22. "Busy times happen, and we're here to help. Let's take it one step at a time with a gradual approach."

23. "Time is of the essence, and we respect that. Let's keep it practical and efficient."

24. "I understand; you're right in the thick of it. Let's discuss how our solution can simplify things for you."

25. "Being busy is a sign of success, and we're here to support that. Let's make this transition as seamless as possible."

I have never heard of your company. How do I know if you are legitimate?

1. "I completely understand your concern. We're a reputable company with a strong track record, and we'd be happy to share more about our history and clients."

2. "Not a problem at all. Many successful companies were once unfamiliar. We can provide references and case studies to demonstrate our legitimacy."

3. "I get it; trust is important. We're happy to provide you with our credentials, certifications, and customer reviews to prove our legitimacy."

4. "It's natural to be cautious with new names. We've been in business for [number of years] and have a solid reputation for integrity and quality."

5. "No worries, we all start somewhere. We're backed by numerous satisfied customers who can vouch for our legitimacy."

6. "Being unfamiliar can raise doubts. We'd be glad to provide you with information about our industry awards, affiliations, and past success stories."

7. "I understand your concern. We're a legitimate company, and I can send you information on our background and accomplishments."

8. "I appreciate your diligence. You can check our credentials, online presence, and customer reviews to verify our legitimacy."

9. "It's a valid question. We've successfully served clients in your industry, and I can share some of their experiences with you."

10. "No problem at all. We are a legitimate company, and I can provide you with information on our financial stability and industry reputation."

11. "I respect your skepticism. Feel free to research us online and see what our customers say about our products and services."

12. "I understand your concern. We can provide you with references from clients who have worked with us and can vouch for our legitimacy."

13. "I appreciate your caution. We're a trustworthy company, and I can provide you with our business registration details and any other information you'd like."

14. "It's a common question. We've been in business for [number of years] and have maintained a strong reputation for legitimacy and reliability."

15. "I get it; you want to be sure. Our legitimacy is backed by industry recognition and a strong customer base. We're more than happy to share that with you."

16. "I understand you want to be cautious. We have a proven track record and can provide you with references to verify our legitimacy."

17. "No worries. We have a solid presence in the market and can offer you proof of our legitimacy through customer testimonials and case studies."

18. "It's wise to be cautious. We've received industry awards and are backed by a team of experts who can vouch for our legitimacy."

19. "Your concern is valid. We are a legitimate company, and I can provide you with references and testimonials to back that up."

20. "I respect your due diligence. We have a long history of successful partnerships and satisfied clients who can confirm our legitimacy."

21. "I appreciate your skepticism. You can find information about our company on our website, including case studies and customer testimonials."

22. "I understand the need for reassurance. We're a trustworthy company with a strong presence in our industry. Let's discuss how we can address your concerns."

23. "It's normal to have questions about a new company. I'd be happy to provide you with a portfolio of our work and connect you with existing clients for validation."

24. "Your concern is completely valid. We can share our company's history and success stories to demonstrate our legitimacy."

25. "I respect your caution. We are a legitimate company, and we can offer references and client success stories to assure you of our authenticity."

Switching service providers seems like it is going to be too complicated.

1. "I totally get where you're coming from. We're here to make this whole switch thing as painless as a breeze!"

2. "No worries, we've got a team of pros to handle the nitty-gritty. Your job? Just sit back and enjoy the change."

3. "Switching might seem a bit daunting, but trust us, we're like the GPS for your transition – guiding you all the way!"

4. "You won't be going at it alone. Our support team's got your back, and they're a friendly bunch!"

5. "Complications? Well, that's our cue to shine. We specialize in simplifying stuff for our clients."

6. "We've made our onboarding process so user-friendly that you'll be switching like a pro in no time!"

7. "You're not in this alone. Our support crew is your sidekick through this journey."

8. "We get it – change can be tricky. But once you see the benefits, you'll be high-fiving yourself!"

9. "We've got a tailor-made plan for you to ensure the switch is as smooth as your favorite playlist."

10. "How about we set up a chat to run through the whole process? You can ask anything on your mind."

11. "Complications often happen with outdated systems. We're all about the latest tech to make it easy."

12. "A bit of hassle now, but you'll be thanking yourself in the long run for a more fantastic service."

13. "We've had clients who were a little nervous at first, but they're now our biggest fans!"

14. "Sit back, relax, and let us handle the nitty-gritty. You focus on what you do best – your business."

15. "Our plan ensures zero downtime during the switch. You won't even notice the change happening!"

16. "Think of it as investing in a better future. The short-term hiccups will turn into long-term happiness!"

17. "We've made our systems so user-friendly; you'll wonder why you didn't switch earlier!"

18. "Change is never easy, but we'll be here every step of the way to keep things fun and breezy."

19. "Don't let the switch jitters hold you back from a more epic service experience!"

20. "We've got your back. Let's chat about your unique needs, and we'll make this switch a piece of cake."

21. "Switching can be a little intimidating, but we promise to make it an adventure, not a hassle."

22. "Complications? We'll tackle 'em head-on and make sure you have a stress-free transition."

23. "Our goal is a seamless switch with no fuss. Your business is too important to disrupt."

24. "Our clients have told us switching was a game-changer. It's time to join the winning team!"

25. "Tell me your concerns, and we'll cook up a plan that'll have you switching with a smile. We're here for you!"

These more conversational rebuttals aim to reassure the prospect in a friendly manner, emphasizing your commitment to making the switch hassle-free and enjoyable.

Your competitor has a cheaper price.

1. "I totally get your price concerns. Let's chat about what our product brings to the table in terms of features and support."

2. "Yeah, I've heard that too. But here's the thing – while the other guys might seem cheaper upfront, our product could save you money in the long run because of its quality."

3. "Have you had a chance to really compare what both products offer? Price is just a piece of the puzzle."

4. "Let's talk about your budget and what you need. Maybe we can find something that fits your wallet."

5. "It's pretty common to see lower prices out there. However, our product is all about better quality and performance."

6. "We can break it down and talk about all the costs, including maintenance and support, so you can see the bigger picture."

7. "We're big on providing awesome customer service, which can actually save you time and money in the long run."

8. "I get that price is on your mind, but here's the scoop – our solution has a reputation for being reliable and top-notch."

9. "A lot of folks choose us for our track record, even if we're not the absolute cheapest option. It's because we deliver where it counts."

10. "You're right to be cautious about hidden costs. Let's make sure you're getting all the features and support you need."

11. "We totally get the need to stay within budget. Let's see if we can cook up a pricing plan that works for you."

12. "Our solution offers some unique perks that can make your work smoother and save you some cash."

13. "Cheaper doesn't always mean better, right? Let's dig into the extra benefits you'll get with our solution."

14. "I understand your concerns. It's important to make sure you're not sacrificing what you need for a lower price."

15. "Our clients often find that our solution is like a money-making machine because of its performance."

16. "Give me the lowdown on your needs, and we can probably find a solution that fits your budget."

17. "Our pricing is all about getting you the best bang for your buck. We want you to be happy with your investment."

18. "We're flexible with our pricing. Let's figure out a plan that works for your wallet and your needs."

19. "I appreciate your due diligence. Let's see if we can make our pricing jive with your business."

20. "Yeah, price is important, but it's not the whole story. Our reputation and the value we bring to the table matter just as much. What's most important to you?"

I can't afford this right now. But I should be able to later down the road.

1. "I appreciate your honesty about your current situation. Let's discuss how we can make it work in the future."

2. "No problem! We understand budgets can be tight. How about we explore some flexible options for you down the road?"

3. "We're here to help. Let's keep the conversation open so that when the time is right, we can get you started."

4. "I completely understand your financial concerns. Let's plan for a future date that works better for you."

5. "It's great that you're considering our offering for the future. We'll be here when you're ready."

6. "Your financial well-being is important. We can explore different plans or promotions when you're ready."

7. "We don't want you to stretch yourself too thin. Let's keep in touch and revisit this when it's more convenient."

8. "No worries, life's full of changes. When you're in a better position, we'll be here to help you get started."

9. "Your honesty is appreciated. Let's work together to find a solution that fits your budget in the future."

10. "I understand you can't commit right now. Let's discuss a timeline that aligns better with your financial goals."

11. "Financial situations can change. We'll be ready to assist you whenever you're ready to move forward."

12. "Affordability is crucial. We can stay in touch and revisit your options when it's more comfortable for you."

13. "When you're ready, we'll make it work for your budget. In the meantime, we're here to answer any questions."

14. "Thank you for considering us for the future. We'll keep the conversation alive and ready to assist when you are."

15. "Let's keep the door open for a future collaboration. When the time is right, we'll be eager to assist."

16. "We'll respect your current financial situation and revisit this when you're in a better place to move forward."

17. "Don't worry about it. We're patient and will be here when you're in a more comfortable financial position."

18. "Your financial well-being is a top priority for us. We can discuss options when the timing is right for you."

19. "Affordability is key. Let's find a solution that aligns with your financial goals when the time is right."

20. "We're in this for the long term. When you're ready, we'll be here to help you achieve your goals."

21. "Your future interest is important to us. We can keep the conversation going and assist you at the right time."

22. "Life happens, and we understand. Let's reconnect when your financial situation allows for it."

23. "We're not going anywhere. When you're ready, we'll work together to make this happen."

24. "I appreciate your honesty. Let's stay connected, and when the timing is right, we'll get you started."

25. "Your future business is valuable to us. We'll patiently await the moment when you're ready to make the leap."

Chapter Three: Cold Outreach Scripts and Templates with Responses

Tool One: Outbound Cold Call Scripts

The goal of a cold outreach is very similar to the goal of a good response, with the added goal of making a decision maker aware of your products and services.

1. Make a decision maker aware of your products and services,

2. Get the prospect's permission to continue talking,

3. Give your elevator speech (Features + Benefits + Consequences),

4. Gather data you need to offer your product or service,

5. Schedule an appointment if you can't gather data right now, or

6. Get a priority contact date so you know when the conversation will be important to the prospect. (The date the product or service ends, runs out, is needed again, and the contact's birthday!)

Below I am going to give you a few examples of cold outreach scripts with example prospect responses. Simply modify the cold outreach script to match your products and services.

Example One: Commercial Insurance Cold Call Script

"Hi, my name is _____ and I'm calling with the Williams Family Investment and Insurance Group.

How are you today?

I would like to speak with the person who handles the business insurance policies for your company if an insurance claim needed to be filed, would that be you? _____ "

Prospect says: "They are not in right now."

Your Response: "No problem, I will call back. Who should I ask for, and what is the best time to call back to reach them?"

Prospect Says: "I am the person you need to talk to. What is this about?"

Your Response: "Who am I speaking with? [First Name], I am calling on behalf of the Williams Family Insurance Agency, we offer Commercial Insurance and Risk Management Services to Businesses like yours.

It will take me 30 seconds to share with you what we can do for you . . . and if anything sparks your interest, we can keep talking. Will you give me 30 seconds?

If "no", say "I understand I caught you at a busy time. What is the best time that I can call back and steal a few minutes of your day to try and compete for your business insurance?"

If "Yes. I am the person that handles the insurance":

Great! Again, I am with the Williams Family Investment and Insurance Agency. We are a Certified Risk Management agency which specializes in auditing your present commercial insurance policies, checking how they compares to the needs of your business, and looking for gaps in coverage which expose your company to unnecessary risk and out of pocket expenses.

Businesses choose us as an Insurance Agency for three main reasons:

First, businesses are concerned that their insurance gets more expensive every year, and they don't understand why, and rarely get an explanation of why their insurance increased, and they are often too busy to look for other insurance options, so they just renew every year.

Second, businesses are bothered by the fact that their current Insurance Provider does not give them the attention they once did.

Third, many companies are frustrated because the last time they had a claim, it did not go so well.

Did you hear any reason from these 3 points that would concern you and your company?

If Yes: Okay. . . What did you hear that Raises Concerns for you?

If "No or not interested":

[First Name], our research shows that your insurance is coming up for renewal soon *[Exact Date if you have it.]* and, it is always a great idea to get a second opinion by having a competitor look at your current policy. We want to compete for your business, so we will find any weaknesses or problems and point them out to you.

By getting a second opinion you will either learn about problems you don't currently know exist, or you will get confirmation that you have the best policy for you.

All I need is some basic information and 10 minutes of your time. Can I give you a second opinion on your commercial insurance policy?

If "Yes" Complete the Fact Finder

If "No" "I understand that right now you are comfortable with your current insurance, but insurance prices fluctuate every year, so I will try back as your insurance comes up for renewal. When does your current policy expire? What Company are you with?"

Example Cold Call Outreach Scripts with Appointment Request

1. Introduction Script with Elevator Speech and Appointment Request:

- Hi, this is [Your Name] from [Your Company]. I hope I'm not catching you at a bad time. We specialize in [Insert Elevator Pitch]. I'd love to learn more about your needs and see if our [product/service] could be a valuable solution for your company. Can we schedule a quick 15-minute call to discuss this further?

2. Value Proposition Script with Elevator Speech and Appointment Request:

- Hi there, I'm [Your Name] with [Your Company]. We help businesses like yours [solve a specific problem or achieve a particular goal, e.g., "improve customer retention" or "streamline operations"]. In fact, our [product/service] has [briefly mention a unique benefit]. I'd like to discuss how this could be a game-changer for your business. Can we set up a 15-minute call to explore this?

3. Curiosity Script with Elevator Speech and Appointment Request:

- Hello, this is [Your Name] calling from [Your Company]. We've recently helped a few businesses in your industry boost their [key metric, e.g., "revenue by 30%"]. Our secret sauce is our [briefly describe a key feature or strategy, e.g., "AI-powered analytics"]. I'd like to share how we did it and see if it might make sense for you. How about scheduling a 15-minute call to dive into this?

4. Industry Insight Script with Elevator Speech and Appointment Request:

- Hey, it's [Your Name] from [Your Company]. I've been following your industry closely and noticed a trend related to [industry-specific topic, e.g., "the shift toward sustainability"]. Our [product/service] is designed to help companies like yours stay ahead in this changing landscape. How about we set up a brief call to discuss how this could benefit your business?

5. Problem-Solution Script with Elevator Speech and Appointment Request:

- Hi, I'm [Your Name] with [Your Company]. Many businesses are struggling with [common industry problem, e.g., "inventory management inefficiencies"], and we've developed a solution that can make a significant difference. Our [product/service] is designed to [briefly describe the solution, e.g., "streamline your inventory processes"]. Would you be open to a 15-minute call to explore how it could work for your company?

6. Benefit-Focused Script with Elevator Speech and Appointment Request:

- This is [Your Name] from [Your Company]. Our [product/service] has been proven to [deliver a specific benefit, e.g., "increase sales by 25%"] for companies similar to yours. It's a game-changer. Can we schedule a quick 15-minute call so I can share more about how it can impact your business?

7. Customer Success Story Script with Elevator Speech and Appointment Request:

- Hi there, I'm [Your Name] with [Your Company]. We recently worked with [Customer's Name], and they saw remarkable results after implementing our [product/service]. In fact, they [mention the specific success, e.g., "doubled their online traffic"]. Would you be open to a 15-minute call to discuss how our solution might help you achieve similar results?

8. Competition Comparison Script with Elevator Speech and Appointment Request:

- Hello, this is [Your Name] from [Your Company]. We've found that businesses like yours are choosing our [product/service] over [Competitor's Name] because of [specific differentiator, e.g., "better pricing and more features"]. It's a no-brainer. How about we schedule a quick 15-minute call to explore how our solution outperforms the competition?

9. Trial Offer Script with Elevator Speech and Appointment Request:

- Hi, I'm [Your Name] with [Your Company]. We're so confident in the value of our [product/service] that we offer a no-obligation trial. It's a risk-free way to see how it can benefit your company. Would you be interested in scheduling a 15-minute call to discuss how the trial works and explore if it's a good fit for you?

10. Follow-Up Script with Elevator Speech and Appointment Request:

- Hi, this is [Your Name] again from [Your Company]. I wanted to follow up on our previous conversation and see if you've had a chance to consider how our [product/service] might fit into your plans. How about we set up a 15-minute call to revisit this and address any questions or concerns you might have?

Tool Two: Outbound Cold Voicemail Scripts

1. General Introduction:

- Hi, it's [Your Name] from [Your Company]. We've got some really cool stuff to help businesses like yours. Let's chat about how our [product/service] can boost your business. Can we set up a quick call? Chat soon!

2. Value Proposition:

- Hey there, I'm [Your Name] with [Your Company]. We're all about helping businesses like yours [solve a specific problem or achieve a particular goal, e.g., "boost sales" or "improve efficiency"]. Our [product/service] can really make a difference for you. How about we connect for a quick chat? Are you available?

3. Curiosity Approach:

- Hi, this is [Your Name] calling from [Your Company]. We've been working with companies in your industry and achieving some incredible results. I'd love to share how we did it and see if it could work for you. Can we set up a brief call to dive into this?

4. Industry Insight:

- Hi, it's [Your Name] from [Your Company]. I've been keeping an eye on your industry and noticed a cool trend related to [industry-specific topic, e.g., "the shift toward sustainability"]. Our [product/service] is designed to keep businesses like yours ahead of the curve. How about we set up a quick call to chat about this?

5. Problem-Solution:

- Hello, it's [Your Name] from [Your Company]. Many businesses are dealing with [common industry problem, e.g., "inventory management inefficiencies"], and we've got a solution that can help. Our [product/service] is designed to [briefly describe the solution, e.g., "streamline your inventory processes"]. Can we set up a quick call to explore how it could work for your company?

6. Benefit-Focused:

- Hey there, it's [Your Name] with [Your Company]. Our [product/service] has been known to [deliver a specific benefit, e.g., "increase sales by 25%"] for companies like yours. It's a game-changer. I'd love to share more about how it can impact your business. Can we connect for a quick call?

7. Customer Success Story:

- Hi, this is [Your Name] from [Your Company]. We recently worked with [Customer's Name], and they saw amazing results after using our [product/service]. They even [mention the specific success, e.g., "doubled their online traffic"]. Would you be up for a quick chat to discuss how our solution might help you achieve similar results?

8. Competition Comparison:

- Hi, I'm [Your Name] from [Your Company]. We're finding that businesses like yours are choosing our [product/service] over [Competitor's Name] because we offer [specific differentiator, e.g., "better pricing and more features"]. It's a no-brainer. Can we schedule a quick call to explore how our solution is outperforming the competition?

9. Trial Offer:

- Hi, it's [Your Name] with [Your Company]. We're so confident in the value of our [product/service] that we offer a no-obligation trial. It's a risk-free way to see how it can benefit your company. Would you be interested in scheduling a brief call to discuss how the trial works and explore if it's a good fit for you?

10. Follow-Up:

- Hi, this is [Your Name] again from [Your Company]. I wanted to follow up on our previous conversation and see if you've had a chance to think about how our [product/service] might fit into your plans. How about we set up a quick call to revisit this and address any questions or concerns you might have?

11. Data-Driven Approach:

- Hey there, it's [Your Name] from [Your Company]. We're all about data and insights. Our [product/service] can help businesses like yours make smarter decisions and boost profits. Let's chat. Can we set up a quick call? Talk to you soon!

12. Innovative Solutions:

- Hi, it's [Your Name] with [Your Company]. We're known for innovative solutions that can transform the way your business operates. Our [product/service] can be a real game-changer for you. How about we connect for a quick chat? Are you available?

13. Cost Savings:

- Hi, this is [Your Name] calling from [Your Company]. We totally get the importance of cost savings. Our [product/service] has helped businesses like yours cut costs significantly. I'd love to share more about this. When can we hop on a call to discuss it?

14. Proven Track Record:

- Hi, it's [Your Name] with [Your Company]. We've got a track record of helping businesses succeed. Our [product/service] has delivered impressive results for companies in your industry. How about we connect for a quick chat to explore how we can do the same for you?

15. Targeted Marketing:

- Hi there, it's [Your Name] from [Your Company]. Our [product/service] is all about targeted marketing strategies that can skyrocket your brand's visibility. It's an exciting opportunity. Can we schedule a quick call to dive into how it can benefit your business?

16. Streamlined Operations:

- Hey there, I'm [Your Name] with [Your Company]. We specialize in streamlining operations for businesses like yours. Our [product/service] can make your processes more efficient and cost-effective. When can we set up a quick call to explore this further?

17. Revenue Growth:

- Hey, it's [Your Name] from [Your Company]. We're experts in driving revenue growth. Our [product/service] has a proven track record of helping businesses like yours achieve remarkable sales growth. Can we connect for a quick chat to discuss this opportunity?

18. Employee Productivity:

- Hi, this is [Your Name] calling from [Your Company]. We understand the importance of employee productivity. Our [product/service] has shown impressive results in this area. How about we schedule a quick call to explore how it can benefit your business?

19. Customization:

- Hi, it's [Your Name] from [Your Company]. We understand that every business is unique. Our [product/service] is highly customizable to meet your specific needs. Would you be open to a quick call to discuss how we can tailor it to your requirements?

20. Compliance and Security:

- Hi, this is [Your Name] from [Your Company]. We take compliance and security seriously. Our [product/service] ensures your business remains secure and compliant. Can we schedule a quick call to discuss how we can provide peace of mind for your company?

21. Sustainability:

- Hey, it's [Your Name] from [Your Company]. Sustainability is more important than ever. Our [product/service] helps businesses like yours reduce their environmental footprint. How about we connect for a quick call to explore how you can contribute to a more sustainable future?

22. Staff Training:

- Hey there, it's [Your Name] from [Your Company]. Our [product/service] includes comprehensive staff training. It's a valuable resource to improve your team's skills. When can we set up a quick call to discuss how this can benefit your business?

23. Content Marketing:

- Hi, this is [Your Name] from [Your Company]. We're experts in content marketing. Our [product/service] can help your business gain more visibility and engagement. Can we schedule a quick call to explore how it can enhance your brand's presence?

24. Employee Engagement:

- Hey, it's [Your Name] from [Your Company]. We understand the importance of engaged employees. Our [product/service] has shown impressive results in increasing employee engagement. Would you be open to a quick call to discuss how this can positively impact your business?

25. Customer Service Enhancement:

- Hi, it's [Your Name] from [Your Company]. We're all about delivering exceptional customer service. Our [product/service] can help you take customer satisfaction to the next level. Can we set up a quick call to discuss how it can benefit your business and enhance your customer relationships?

Tool Three: Cold Outreach Email Templates with Elevator Pitch and Appointment Request

Opening cold outreach emails with consequences produces better open rates, read rates, and engagement.

1. Introduction and Value Proposition:

Subject: [Company Name}'s commercial insurance is about to expire on (Expiration Date]

Hey [Prospect's Name],

Not jumping on board with this could mean falling behind your competitors.

Hope you're doing awesome! I wanted to give you the lowdown on [Your Company], where we're all about helping businesses like yours.

Our [product/service] is a game-changer. It's like having a secret sauce that makes businesses [benefit]. Not jumping on board with this could mean missing out big time.

How about we grab a quick chat next week? I promise it's worth your time!

Cheers,

[Your Name]

[Your Title]

[Your Company]

[Your Contact Information]

2. Data-Driven Solutions:

Subject: Data Magic: Make Your Business Awesome with [Your Company]!

Hey [Prospect's Name],

At [Your Company], we're all about data and insights – the good stuff that makes businesses tick. Our [product/service] will have your team making genius, data-driven decisions that lead to [benefit].

Not grabbing this opportunity could mean missing out big time. How about we set up a quick chat to make your business shine?

Catch you on the flip side,

[Your Name]

[Your Title]

[Your Company]

[Your Contact Information]

3. Innovative Solutions:

Subject: Unleash the Magic of Innovation with [Your Company]!

Hey [Prospect's Name],

We're all about shaking things up and making your business more efficient. Our [product/service] is the answer you've been looking for to kick things into high gear.

Missing out on this could mean falling behind your competitors. How about we set up a quick chat and see how we can make your business run like a well-oiled machine?

Excited to chat soon,

[Your Name]

[Your Title]

[Your Company]

[Your Contact Information]

4. Cost Savings Opportunity:

Subject: Crush Your Costs with [Your Company]!

Hey [Prospect's Name],

We get it – saving costs is a big deal. At [Your Company], we're all about helping businesses like yours achieve massive cost savings.

Not jumping on this opportunity could mean missing out big time. How about we set up a quick chat to explore the world of cost savings?

Catch you on the cost-saving side,

[Your Name]

[Your Title]

[Your Company]

[Your Contact Information]

5. Proven Track Record:

Subject: Success Stories Await You with [Your Company]!

Hey [Prospect's Name],

At [Your Company], we've got a solid track record of helping businesses succeed. Our [product/service] consistently delivers impressive results.

Not partnering with us could mean missing out big time. Let's chat about how we can create your success story together.

Excited to chat soon,

[Your Name]

[Your Title]

[Your Company]

[Your Contact Information]

6. Streamlined Operations:

Subject: Making Business Easier with [Your Company]!

Hey [Prospect's Name],

Streamlining operations is where the magic happens. At [Your Company], we're all about making your processes more efficient and cost-effective.

Not optimizing could mean missing out big time. How about we set up a quick chat to explore the world of business ease?

Looking forward to making your life easier,

[Your Name]

[Your Title]

[Your Company]

[Your Contact Information]

7. Revenue Growth Potential:

Subject: Skyrocket Your Sales with [Your Company]!

Hey [Prospect's Name],

We're the experts when it comes to boosting sales and helping businesses thrive. Our [product/service] consistently drives remarkable sales growth.

Not hopping on this opportunity could mean missing out big time. How about we set up a quick chat to discuss your path to sales success?

Looking forward to making your business rock,

[Your Name]

[Your Title]

[Your Company]

[Your Contact Information]

8. Employee Productivity:

Subject: Supercharge Your Team with [Your Company]!

Hey [Prospect's Name],

Engaged employees are the secret sauce to business success. At [Your Company], we've got a recipe to make it happen. Our [product/service] pumps up employee productivity like nobody's business.

Not seizing this opportunity could mean missing out big time. How about we set up a quick chat and level up your team's game?

Excited to chat soon,

[Your Name]

[Your Title]

[Your Company]

[Your Contact Information]

9. Sustainable Practices:

Subject: Join the Green Revolution with [Your Company]!

Hey [Prospect's Name],

Sustainability is the name of the game. At [Your Company], we help businesses like yours reduce their environmental footprint with our [product/service].

Not joining the green movement could mean missing out big time. How about we set up a quick chat to make your business more eco-friendly?

Catch you on the green side,

[Your Name]

[Your Title]

[Your Company]

[Your Contact Information]

10. Customized Solutions:

Subject: Custom-Made Solutions Await You at [Your Company]!

Hey [Prospect's Name],

We get it – every business is unique. That's why at [Your Company], we offer super-customizable [product/service] solutions designed just for your needs. Not customizing could mean missing out big time.

How about we set up a quick chat to tailor our offerings to your unique requirements?

Looking forward to making your life easier,

[Your Name]

[Your Title]

[Your Company]

[Your Contact Information]

Commercial Insurance X-Date Focused Cold Outreach Email

Subject: [Company Name}'s commercial insurance is about to expire on (Expiration Date]

"Hi [Lead's Name], it's Billy Williams from the Williams Family Insurance and Investment Group. Our research shows that your current commercial insurance is about to expire.

Appointment Calendar Link: https://calendly.com/wfig

We've helped many [Type of Profession] find the best commercial insurance coverage.

Because we are an independent agency, we have over 20 Insurance companies that we shop so we can find the best insurance for your company.

We only need about 10 minutes and some basic information about your company, and we can start talking to our carriers on your behalf.

I will provide my appointment link so you can find a day and time that works best for you, and I can get the information I need to start working on your quote: https://calendly.com/wfig

Billy R. Williams, Ph.D.

Contact me by phone at 682-206-3836,

By email at billy@williamsinvgroup.com,

By text message at 682-206-3836, or

For an instant commercial insurance quote, visit our website at wfig.info.

Again, contact me by phone at 682-206-3836, by email at billy@williamsinvgroup.com, by text message at 682-206-3836, or for an instant commercial insurance quote, visit our website at wfig.info.

Tool Four: Permission-Based Outbound Marketing Text Message Templates

It is extremely important that you only send permission-based text messages. The best ways to guarantee that text messages are permission based is for the prospect to text you or your company first, or you have an opt in option on all landing pages, websites, and forms.

1. Hey! Boost sales with [Product/Service] at [Your Website]. It's a game-changer!

2. I just sent you an email about [Product/Service]. Check spam if you don't see it.

3. Here is a video about [Product/Service]. Schedule an appt. right on the video!

4. Ready to up your game? Try our [Product/Service] now! [Your Website]

5. Save big on costs with [Product/Service]. Check it out at [Your Website].

6. Make things smoother with [Product/Service]. Let's talk soon!

7. Grow your biz with [Product/Service]. It's a game-changer. Interested?

8. Let's chat about [Product/Service] Text or call me back

9. Streamline ops with [Product/Service]. Find out more at [Your Website].

10. Ready for more profits? Explore [Product/Service] today.

11. Turbocharge your service with [Product/Service]. Interested?

12. Skyrocket sales with [Product/Service]. Ready to chat more?

13. Get eco-friendly with [Product/Service]. Learn more at [Your Website].

14. Open doors to innovation with [Product/Service]. Let's chat!

15. Tailored solutions: [Product/Service]. Ready to talk?

16. Boost productivity with [Product/Service]. Interested?

17. Get data-driven insights with [Product/Service]. Want to know more?

18. Transform your biz with [Product/Service]. Let's chat soon!

19. [Product/Service] = Success. Learn more about it today!

20. Sustainable growth? Try [Product/Service]. Interested?

21. Game-changing solutions: [Product/Service]. Let's chat!

22. Customized success with [Product/Service]. Interested to talk?

23. Fuel revenue growth with [Product/Service]. Curious?

24. Quick chat about [Product/Service]? Interested to know more?

25. [Product/Service] makes life easier. Let's chat soon!

26. Learn more about [Product/Service] at [Your Website]. Interested?

Tool Five: Cold Outreach Social Networking Direct Message Templates

1. "Hey there! Our [Product/Service] lets you order groceries online, saving time and hassle. Missing out might mean more trips to the store. Can we discuss further? You can reach me at [Your Contact Information]."

2. "Ready to upgrade your home entertainment? Our [Product/Service] offers a wide range of shows and movies, leading to endless entertainment. Let's connect for a quick chat! My availability is [Your Availability]."

3. "Time to simplify your meal prep! Our [Product/Service] provides meal kits with easy-to-follow recipes, which means fewer cooking frustrations. Ignoring this may lead to more time spent in the kitchen. How about a conversation? You can reach me at [Your Contact Information]."

4. "Elevate your skincare with our [Product/Service]! Featuring all-natural ingredients, it promises healthier skin. Failing to seize this opportunity could mean missed glow-up days. Let's schedule a time to chat. How's your availability?"

5. "Ready for a wardrobe update? Our [Product/Service] can transform your style with personalized fashion recommendations, leading to a trendy look. Not embracing this may result in outdated fashion choices. When are you free for a quick call?"

6. "Enhance your workout with [Product/Service]. It comes with personalized fitness plans, promising improved health and fitness. Neglecting this could lead to stagnant fitness goals. Can we discuss this in more detail? My availability is [Your Availability]."

7. "Revamp your beauty routine with [Product/Service]. It's designed to boost your skincare routine, which can mean healthier, radiant skin. Ignoring this may result in missed self-care opportunities. How about we talk? You can reach me at [Your Contact Information]."

8. "Want to stay organized? Our [Product/Service] features a user-friendly app for tracking tasks, reducing chaos. Failing to embrace this

could result in missed deadlines and appointments. When's a good time for a chat? My availability is [Your Availability]."

9. "Ready for healthier meals? Dive into [Product/Service]. Featuring meal planning, it can lead to a healthier lifestyle. Missing out on this opportunity could mean missed wellness goals. Can we schedule a conversation? You can reach me at [Your Contact Information]."

10. "Elevate your gaming experience with [Product/Service]. It's all about high-quality gaming gear, offering a competitive edge. Neglecting this might lead to missed gaming opportunities. How about we discuss this further? When are you available?"

11. "Drive savings with [Product/Service]. It comes with a budgeting tool for financial control, resulting in more money in your pocket. Not exploring this opportunity may result in more financial stress. Let's chat! My availability is [Your Availability]."

12. "Ready for a fresh look? Our [Product/Service] can make your hair more vibrant with natural hair products, leading to hair goals. Ignoring this could mean more bad hair days. When can we have a quick call?"

13. "Innovation meets convenience with [Product/Service]. Featuring a mobile app for quick shopping, it can mean more free time for you. Neglecting this could result in missed leisure moments. How about we chat further? You can reach me at [Your Contact Information]."

14. "Personalized style for you: [Product/Service]. It's designed to offer fashion suggestions, promising a unique wardrobe. Failing to customize could lead to missed style opportunities. Can we schedule a discussion? When are you available?"

15. "Boost your self-care with [Product/Service]. It's got mindfulness exercises, promising reduced stress. Neglecting this could result in more anxious days. How about we discuss this in more detail? You can reach me at [Your Contact Information]."

Insurance Product Focused Social Networking Direct Message Template

"I am a local insurance agent and I am an expert at insuring (Niche or target prospect). I have solved many insurance related problems for (Insert Profession) in the (Geographic Area).

Please connect with me.

Here is a link to a short video that tells you a little about me: (YouTube or Loom Video Link) and a link to my Appointment Calendar. Please schedule a quick call or video meeting (Appointment Calendar Link)."

Tool Six: Cold Outreach Personalized Video Script

COMMERCIAL INSURANCE VIDEO SCRIPT

Subject: It's time to get a second opinion on your insurance

My name is Billy R. Williams, and I am the president of the Williams Family Insurance and Investment Group. (WFIG)

We specialize in providing comprehensive commercial insurance that protects every aspect of your business.

In today's ever-changing commercial insurance landscape, defending your business from lawsuits, protecting equipment and property that your business owns, protecting your employees and contract labor, as well as managing your insurance premiums are extremely important items.

We offer insurance packages designed to meet the unique needs of your businesses.

Unfortunately, most business leaders are so busy running the business that they wait until the last minute to think about insurance and just automatically renew with the current agency.

This could mean thousands of dollars of lost savings as well as their insurance coverage not keeping up with the changes in the business.

I'd love to compete for your commercial insurance business, and I welcome the opportunity to discuss how our expertise can benefit your organization.

To make this process simple for both of us, I am going to give you several options to contact me and my team so you can learn more about our agency and why you should allow us to compete for your commercial insurance business.

You can schedule a phone or video meeting on a day and time that works best for you by using the appointment calendar link: https://calendly.com/wfig;

You can reach us by phone at 682-206-3836 (Use the Commercial Insurance Prompt)

You can email me directly at billy@williamsinvgroup.com

You can text message us at 682-206-3836 and one of my team will call you back as soon as possible.

Visit our website and read some of our reviews and testimonials at: https://www.wfig.info/

What ever way you decide to reach us, you will be glad you did!

Thank you for your time!

Billy R. Williams

President - Williams Family Insurance and Investment Group

Appointment Calendar Link: https://calendly.com/wfig

Introduction Video Script for a Home-Based Ecommerce Business

[INTRODUCTION]

Narrator (enthusiastic tone, showcasing home-based entrepreneurs): "Welcome to [Your Home-Based E-Commerce Business] - where your shopping experience meets entrepreneurship! If you're a savvy shopper looking for unique products while supporting local businesses, you're in for a treat."

[CONSUMER-FRIENDLY MARKETPLACE]

Visuals (showing a user-friendly e-commerce platform): "At [Your Home-Based E-Commerce Business], we've created a consumer-friendly marketplace that caters to your needs. Whether you're looking for handcrafted goods, exclusive fashion, or innovative gadgets, you'll find it here."

[EXCLUSIVE FINDS]

Narrator (confidence in voice, with visuals of unique products): "We understand your desire for the extraordinary. That's why we bring you a curated selection of exclusive finds - items you won't find in traditional stores. From handmade jewelry to limited-edition artwork, we've got it all."

[SUPPORTING LOCAL ENTREPRENEURS]

Visuals (showing small business owners at work): "But there's more to our platform than just great products. When you shop with us, you're supporting local entrepreneurs. Our home-based business owners pour their hearts and souls into their creations."

[SHOPPING MADE EASY]

Narrator (warm and reassuring): "We've designed our platform to make your shopping experience as easy as possible. You can browse, compare, and purchase from the comfort of your home, knowing you're getting top-quality products."

[CUSTOMER REVIEWS]

Visuals (showing positive customer reviews): "Don't just take our word for it - our satisfied customers have plenty to say."

Customer 1 (enthusiastic): "I love the unique products I've found at [Your Home-Based E-Commerce Business]. The quality and customer service are outstanding."

Customer 2 (happy): "It feels great to support local entrepreneurs while getting exceptional products. I've had nothing but positive experiences with this platform."

[SAFE & SECURE]

Narrator (emphasizing security): "We take your online safety seriously. Our platform is equipped with state-of-the-art security features to ensure your transactions are safe and secure."

[PERSONALIZED SHOPPING]

Visuals (showing a customized shopping experience): "Personalization is key to our platform. We use your preferences to recommend products that match your style and interests. It's like having a personal shopper at your fingertips."

[CALL TO ACTION]

Narrator (energetic): "Are you ready to discover the magic of shopping with a purpose? Join [Your Home-Based E-Commerce Business] today and experience the joy of unique finds while supporting local entrepreneurs!"

[SPECIAL OFFER & CONTACT INFORMATION]

Visuals (displaying contact details and special offers): "For a limited time, enjoy a special offer: [Mention offer details]. Don't miss the chance to shop with a purpose. Contact us now at [Phone Number] or visit our website at [Your Website]."

[CONCLUSION]

Narrator (with enthusiasm and visuals of consumers shopping online): "At [Your Home-Based E-Commerce Business], we're dedicated to providing you with an unforgettable shopping experience while supporting small business owners. Thank you for choosing us as your go-to online marketplace. We look forward to bringing more unique finds your way!"

[OUTRO]

Visuals (showing shoppers and entrepreneurs celebrating): "Shop with purpose today at [Your Home-Based E-Commerce Business]. Make the smart choice for unique products and supporting local entrepreneurs. Contact us now!"

[END OF VIDEO]

Introduction Video Script for a Beauty Shop

[Introduction]

Narrator (with enthusiasm, showing visuals of a beauty shop exterior): "Welcome to [Your Beauty Shop]! If you're looking to elevate your beauty game, you've come to the right place. We're excited to introduce you to a world of self-care and transformation!"

[BEAUTY TRANSFORMATION]

Visuals (showing before-and-after transformations of customers): "At [Your Beauty Shop], we believe that everyone deserves to look and feel their best. Our team of skilled professionals is dedicated to enhancing your natural beauty, taking you from 'everyday' to 'extraordinary'."

[EXPERT TEAM]

Narrator (confidence in voice, with visuals of talented beauty experts): "Our team is made up of experienced and highly trained beauty experts who are passionate about making you shine. They're not just experts; they're artists who use their talent to bring out the best in you."

[SERVICES OFFERED]

Visuals (showing a variety of beauty services): "From hair styling and coloring to makeup, nails, and skincare, we offer a wide range of services that cater to your unique beauty needs. Our goal is to make you feel pampered and confident."

[THE ULTIMATE PAMPERING EXPERIENCE]

Narrator (warm and inviting): "When you step into [Your Beauty Shop], you're not just a customer; you're our guest. Our mission is to provide you with the ultimate pampering experience. From the moment you arrive, we ensure you feel relaxed and rejuvenated."

[ECO-FRIENDLY AND PREMIUM PRODUCTS]

Visuals (showing eco-friendly and premium beauty products): "We care about your well-being and the environment. That's why we use eco-friendly and premium products that enhance your beauty without compromising on quality or safety."

[CUSTOMER SATISFACTION]

Narrator (emphasizing customer satisfaction): "Your satisfaction is our top priority. We've had the privilege of serving countless delighted customers who have seen incredible results. But don't just take our word for it; listen to what they have to say."

Customer 1 (smiling): "I always leave [Your Beauty Shop] with a smile on my face. Their stylists are fantastic, and I've never felt more beautiful!"

Customer 2 (satisfied): "I've struggled with skincare for years, but [Your Beauty Shop] completely transformed my skin. I can't thank them enough."

[THE ART OF MAKEUP]

Visuals (showing makeup artists at work): "Makeup is an art, and our makeup artists are true artists. They know how to highlight your best features and create the perfect look for any occasion."

[SELF-CARE & WELLNESS]

Narrator (emphasizing self-care): "Self-care is not just about beauty; it's about wellness too. We offer relaxation and rejuvenation services to help you de-stress and recharge."

[CALL TO ACTION]

Narrator (energetic): "Are you ready to experience the beauty transformation of a lifetime? Book an appointment at [Your Beauty Shop] and discover the magic of self-care! Say goodbye to ordinary and hello to extraordinary!"

[SPECIAL OFFER & CONTACT INFORMATION]

Visuals (displaying contact details and special offers): "For a limited time, take advantage of our special offer: [Mention offer details]. Don't miss this opportunity to elevate your beauty game. Contact us now at [Phone Number] or visit our website at [Your Website]."

[CONCLUSION]

Narrator (with enthusiasm and visuals of happy customers): "At [Your Beauty Shop], we're not just in the business of beauty; we're in the business of making you feel confident, pampered, and beautiful. Thank you for considering us as your beauty destination. We can't wait to be a part of your transformation journey!"

[OUTRO]

Visuals (showing a refreshed, confident clientele): "Elevate your beauty game today with [Your Beauty Shop]. Make the smart choice for self-care and confidence. Contact us now!"

[END OF VIDEO]

Intro Video Script for a Carpet Cleaning Service

[Introduction]

"Are your carpets in desperate need of some TLC? Stains, spills, and odors taking over? Don't fret, because we're here to make your carpets look and feel brand new! Introducing [Your Carpet Cleaning Service] – your trusted partner in carpet restoration."

[SHOWCASE OF DIRTY CARPETS]

Visuals (showing before-and-after shots of dirty carpets): "We know how life can take a toll on your carpets. Daily foot traffic, accidental spills, and pet messes can leave your once-lovely carpets looking tired and worn out. But worry not, because we're here to bring back the freshness!"

[EXPERTISE AND EXPERIENCE]

Narrator (confidence in voice, with visuals of skilled technicians): "With years of experience and a team of expert technicians, we've mastered the art of carpet cleaning. We're not just about cleaning; we're about restoring and rejuvenating your carpets to their former glory."

[ADVANCED CLEANING TECHNOLOGY]

Visuals (showing high-tech cleaning equipment): "Our state-of-the-art cleaning technology is the secret behind our success. We use environmentally friendly solutions and cutting-edge equipment to provide a deep and thorough clean. Say goodbye to those stubborn stains and unpleasant odors!"

[CARPET RESTORATION]

Narrator (warm and reassuring): "At [Your Carpet Cleaning Service], we understand that your carpets hold memories and comfort. That's why our mission is to bring your carpets back to life, making your home a comfortable and welcoming place once again."

[CUSTOMER SATISFACTION]

Visuals (showing happy customers): "Our dedication to customer satisfaction is what sets us apart. We take pride in delivering results that exceed your expectations. But don't just take our word for it; listen to what some of our delighted customers have to say."

Customer 1 (smiling): "I couldn't believe my eyes when I saw my carpets after [Your Carpet Cleaning Service] had worked their magic. It was like getting a brand-new carpet without the cost!"

Customer 2 (satisfied): "I've tried DIY cleaning solutions, but nothing compares to the professional touch [Your Carpet Cleaning Service] provided. My carpets feel and smell amazing."

[ECO-FRIENDLY APPROACH]

Narrator (emphasizing eco-friendliness): "We're not just committed to your carpets; we're committed to the environment too. Our cleaning solutions are eco-friendly, ensuring a safe and healthy living space for you and your loved ones."

[CONVENIENCE]

Visuals (showing easy scheduling and quick service): "We understand that your time is precious. That's why we offer hassle-free scheduling and quick service. Your carpets will be fresh, clean, and ready for you in no time."

[CALL TO ACTION]

Narrator (energetic): "Ready to experience the magic of fresh, clean carpets? Contact [Your Carpet Cleaning Service] today and let us work our wonders! Say goodbye to stains, odors, and worn-out carpets. Say hello to a revitalized, comfortable living space!"

[OFFER & CONTACT INFORMATION]

Visuals (displaying contact details and special offers): "For a limited time, take advantage of our special offer: [Mention offer details]. Don't miss this opportunity to give your carpets the care they deserve. Contact us now at [Phone Number] or visit our website at [Your Website]."

[CONCLUSION]

Narrator (with enthusiasm and visuals of pristine carpets): "At [Your Carpet Cleaning Service], we believe that every home deserves beautiful, clean, and fresh carpets. Trust us to bring new life to your carpets. Thank you for considering us as your carpet cleaning partner. We can't wait to make your home a more comfortable and inviting place."

[OUTRO]

Visuals (showing a refreshed, cozy living space): "Transform your home today with [Your Carpet Cleaning Service]. Make the smart choice for your carpets. Contact us now!"

[END OF VIDEO]

Chapter Four: Referral Follow-up Scripts and Templates

Referral Tool One: Phone Call Scripts

Referral Initial Outreach Call Script

Hi [Prospect's Name],

I hope you're doing well. [Referrer's Name] asked me to contact to see if my expertise and experience can help you with [specific business goal or solve a problem you discussed with the referrer].

I am calling to find a good time for a conversation, so I can learn more about what you need.

Do you have a few minutes right now?

(If yes, get information and complete a fact-finder) Ok. Tell me what's going on and then I will ask a couple of questions to make sure I have everything I need to get you taken care of.

(If not, schedule a follow-up appointment.) I have my appointment calendar open, does Tuesday or Wednesday around this time work for you? (Keep working with the referral until you find a time that works best.

I am going to email and text you my contact information and an introductory video that tells you more about me and my company.

What email address should I use?

What phone number should I text? Do me a favor and reply to the text when you get it so I can confirm I have permission to text you and I can add that number to your contact records.

I look forward to helping you with this issue.

Call, email, or text me if you have any questions.

Referral Initial Outreach Call Script (Commercial Insurance Example)

"Hi {Susie}, it's Billy from The Williams Family Insurance and Investment Group Agency.

[Joseph] asked me to contact you and help you solve an issue with the commercial insurance for your company.

My agency specializes in solving insurance problems for business owners and companies, and I am always honored when one of our customers or other professionals we work with, refers our services to other people.

The next step is for us to get some information about the situation so we can choose the best course of action to solve the issue.

Do you have a few minutes right now?

(If yes, get information and complete a fact-finder. See the Inspire a Nation Business Mentoring Commercial Fact Finder: https://www.inspireanation.org/Commercial-Insurance-Marketing)

Ok. Tell me what's going on and then I will ask a couple of questions to make sure I have everything I need to get you taken care of.

(If no, I don't have time right now. schedule a follow-up appointment.)

I have my appointment calendar open, does Tuesday or Wednesday around this time work for you? (Keep working with the referral until you find a time that works best.)

I am going to email and text you the appointment confirmation, and an introductory video that tells you more about me and my company.

What email address should I use?

What phone number should I text?

Do me a favor and reply to the text when you get it so I can confirm I have permission to text you and I can add that number to your contact records.

I look forward to helping you with this issue.

Again, my name is Billy Williams, and I am with the Williams Family Insurance and Investment Group.

My direct phone number is 682-206-3836

Call, email, or text me if you have any questions.

Referral Tool Two: Voicemail Scripts

Referral Voice Mail 1

"Hi. This message is for [Prospect's Name],

I am reaching out because [Referrer's Name] asked me to contact you and assist you with [Product or Service you provide].

[Referrer's Name] gave me your phone number and email address, so I am going to send you an email that has my contact information as well as a text message with a link to a video that tells you about me and my company.

My normal business hours are Monday – Friday 8 AM – 6 PM, and of course, you can text message me when it is convenient for you.

Again, my name is [Your Name] with [Your Company] and I look forward to our conversation. Have an awesome day.

Referral Voice Mail 2

"Hi. This message is for [Prospect's Name],

My name is [Your Name] and I am with [Your Company]. [Referrer's Name] asked me to reach out to you because my expertise is in [Product or Service you provide].

I am looking forward to having a conversation with you.

You can reach me by phone at ???-???-????, again my number is ???-???-????.

You can email me at [Your Email Address] (repeat twice).

Again, my name is [Your Name] with [Your Company]. Please contact me as soon as possible so we can get you taken care of. Take care.

Referral Voice Mail 3

"Hi. This message is for [Prospect's Name],

My name is [Your Name] and I am with [Your Company]. [Referrer's Name] gave me your name, phone, number, and email and asked me to contact you and offer my assistance with [Product or Service you provide].

I am going to email you my contact information and a link to my appointment calendar that you can use to schedule an appointment with me.

I know that emails sometimes end up in a spam folder, so I am also sending a text message to the mobile number [Referrer's Name] gave me for you.

You can call or text me back at ???-???-????, again my number is ???-???-????. This is the same number I used to text you. Thanks [Prospect's Name] for you for your time. I look forward to our conversation. Have a great day.

Referral Tool Three: Email Templates with Appointment Link and Introduction Video

Referral Email Template (Commercial Insurance Example)

"Hi {Mary}, it's Billy from The Williams Family Insurance and Investment Group Agency.

[Joseph] asked me to contact you and help you solve an issue with the commercial insurance for your company.

My agency specializes in solving insurance problems for business owners and companies, and I am always honored when one of our customers or other professionals we work with, refers our services to other people.

The easiest way to meet is for you to schedule a phone or video meeting using the following Appointment Schedule Link: https://calendly.com/wfig/commercial-insurance-15-minute-call-wfig.

During the appointment I will get some information about the situation so we can choose the best course of action to solve the issue.

We only need a few minutes and some basic information about your company, and we can start talking to our carriers on your behalf.

Here are the questions I am going to ask you during our meeting. Please fill out as much of this information as possible prior to the meeting and that will make things go faster and smoother. https://www.wfig.info/wp-content/uploads/sites/248/2023/08/Fillable-082023-WFIG-Commercial-Intake-Form.pdf.

In addition, I am going to leave you several options to contact me as well as a short introduction video so you can put a face on our communication.

You can contact me by phone at 682-206-3836

By email at billy@williamsinvgroup.com

By text message at 682-206-3836.

Introduction Video Link:
https://www.loom.com/share/4893eec704f54345afee5f832dc55d4a?si d=d5f34564-9b2f-4109-8acf-f22a2d510ed0

Referral Email Template (Generic Example)

Hi [Prospect's Name],

I hope you're having an awesome day. [Referrer's Name] mentioned that you're looking for help with [Product or Service you provide] and that there might be a way for me to help out, especially with [specific business goal or a problem].

I'm all about adding value, so I'd love to hear more about what you're up to and see if there's a way I can contribute. When are you free for a quick chat? Let's explore how we can team up to make things happen.

To make scheduling a time to talk simple for you I am providing my appointment calendar link: [Appointment link here]

Here is my contact information and a link to a short video that introduces me and my company.

You can contact me by phone at [???-???-????]

By email at [Your Email Address]

By text message at [???-???-????]

Here is a short video that introduces our business: [Video Link Here]

I look forward to our conversation.

[Your Name]

[Your Company]

[Your Website Address]

Referral Tool Four: Permission Based Outbound Text Message Templates

Referral Text Message 1

"My name is [Your Name] with [Your Company]. [Referrer's Name] asked me to contact you about Product or Service you provide]. Please call me back when you get a chance.

Referral Text Message 2

"Hi [Prospect First Name]. [Referrer's Name] asked me to contact you about [Product or Service you provide]. Here is my appointment calendar link [Insert Link]. Please schedule a quick call.

Referral Text Message 3

"My name is [Your Name] with [Your Company]. [Referrer's Name] asked me to contact you about Product or Service you provide]. Please call me back when you get a chance. Here is a short video that tells you about or company [Intro Video Link]

Referral Text Message 4

"Hi [Prospect First Name]. [Referrer's Name] asked me to contact you about [Product or Service you provide]. Please call or text me back as soon as possible.

Referral Tool Five: Social Networking Direct Message

Social Networking Direct Message 1

"Hi [Prospect First Name]. [Referrer's Name] asked me to contact you about [Product or Service you provide]. [Referrer's Name] expressed to me how eager you were to get this issue taken care of so that's why I am sending you a direct message.

"My name is [Your Name] with [Your Company]. We are experts at solving issues with about [Product or Service you provide].

Our goal is to make sure every customer receives the [Features and Benefits] they deserve, while also making sure that they don't have to deal with the [Consequences] of making a bad decision or waiting too late to make the right decision.

It is important that we talk as soon as possible.

The easiest way to meet is for you to schedule a phone or video meeting using the following Appointment Schedule Link: [Calendar Link Here]

In addition, I am going to leave you several options to contact me, along with a short introduction video so you can put a face on our communication.

You can contact me by phone at [???-???-????]

By email at [Your Email Address]

By text message at [???-???-????]

Here is a short video that introduces our business: [Video Link Here]

I look forward to our conversation.

[Your Name]

[Your Company]

[Your Website Address]

Social Networking Direct Message 2 (Real Estate Agent Example)

"Hi [Dave]. [Maryann] asked me to contact you because [you are looking to relocate to the Dallas area].

[Maryann] expressed to me how eager you were to [find a good real estate agent that could help you] and that's why I found your profile on LinkedIn and I am sending you a direct message.

"My name is [Joe Johnson] with [Top Notch Real Estate]. We are experts at [helping families find the perfect home when they relocate to the Dallas area].

Our goal is to make sure every customer receives the [home and community information, are shown the homes that best fit their desires in their desired price range and are given the time and attention they need to make the best decisions for their family.

Are main goal is making sure that you don't have to deal with the consequences of making the wrong decision and you end up in a house that is

1. Not right for your family

2. Has a crime rating that does not match the quality of life you want for your family.

3. Is in a school district that does not give your child/children the best opportunity to succeed academically,

4. Does not meet your budget.

It is important that we talk as soon as possible.

The easiest way to meet is for you to schedule a phone or video meeting using the following Appointment Schedule Link: [Calendar Link Here]

In addition, I am going to leave you several options to contact me, along with a short introduction video so you can put a face on our communication.

You can contact me by phone at ???-???-????

By email at [Your Email Address]

By text message at ???-???-????

Here is a short video that introduces our business: [Video Link Here]

I look forward to our conversation.

[Your Name]

[Your Company]

[Your Website Address]

Referral Tool Six: Outreach Personalized Video Script

(Note: We use tools such as Zoom, Loom, and Pictory.ai to create videos. Here is a link that will get you 20% off Pictory.ai: https://pictory.ai/?ref=billy16)

Personalized Video (Real Estate Agent Example)

"Hi [Dave]. [Maryann] asked me to contact you because [you are looking to relocate to the Dallas area].

I am sending you this video so you can put a face with this conversation.

[Maryann] expressed to me how eager you were to [find a good real estate agent that could help you].

"My name is [Joe Johnson] with [Top Notch Real Estate]. We are experts at [helping families find the perfect home when they relocate to the Dallas area].

Our goal is to make sure every customer receives the [home and community information that fits their interest, are shown the homes that best fit their desires in their desired price range, and are given the time and attention they need to make the best decisions for their family.]

Are main goal is making sure that you don't have to deal with the consequences of making the wrong decision and you end up in a house that is:

1. Not right for your family

2. Has a crime rating that does not match the quality of life you want for your family.

3. Is in a school district that does not give your child/children the best opportunity to succeed academically,

4. Does not meet your budget.

It is important that we talk as soon as possible.

The easiest way to meet is for you to schedule a phone or video meeting using the following Appointment Schedule Link: [Calendar Link Here]

The appointment link is also located on the top right corner of this video.

This video also allows you to send me a chat message. Just type your chat message in the box that sits below the video.

In addition, I am going to leave you several options to contact me, along with a short introduction video so you can put a face on our communication.

You can contact me by phone at ???-???-????

By email at [Your Email Address]

By text message at ???-???-????

I look forward to our conversation.

[Your Name]

[Your Company]

[Your Website Address]

Chapter 5: Situation Based Responses to Overcome Sales Objection

Example responses for the 5 main areas of the sales cycle where you will most likely face objections.

When initially contacting your lead or prospect.

It's Too Expensive (Insurance Example)

"[First Name], Insurance provides 3 buckets of money when you file a claim, money that is paid directly to you and your family, money that is paid to others on your behalf, and money that is paid to repair or replace the things you have insured.

Without the right insurance in place when you have a claim, you could end up spending thousands of dollars out of pocket instead of spending a few dollars each month to have the right insurance.

I don't know your individual situation, but if you tell me a couple of quick facts, I can give you my professional insight.

Do you have time to have a quick discussion with me right now, or should we find a time that works better for both of us?

Not Interested – (Insurance Example)

"No problem. I don't expect you to be interested yet because I haven't shown you anything that makes your life better.

Give me 60 seconds to give you my pitch and if you are still not interested, I won't waste any more of your time. Is that easy enough?"

When you must leave a voicemail

"Hi. This message is for [Dave]. My name is Billy Williams, and I am with the Williams Family Insurance and Investment Group.

Our records show that your current insurance is about to expire.

Call me when you get this message so we can make sure that when you renew your policy, it is with the best coverage and the best price that you qualify to receive. I know your life is busy, but waiting until the last minute to handle this could make us miss a very important window.

You can call or text me a 682-206-3836, and you can email me at billy@wfig.info.

When trying to gather information from your lead or prospect

I try to make it as easy as possible to do business with me, so here is what I can do, let's schedule an appointment now so we will have a guaranteed date on the calendar, and we can continue to talk for a few minutes until you run out of time and have to go. That should give me enough information to start working on your plan/quote.

When trying to follow-up with your lead or prospect and they won't respond. (Use this as a phone script or email template)

Hello [Prospect's Name], this is Billy Williams with the Williams Family Insurance and Investment Group. I've tried reaching you multiple times through phone calls, emails, and texts to get the information I need to create a quote for your business insurance, and I haven't received a response?

If you are not ready to discuss insurance right now but you still need insurance, reply to one of the ways I am trying to reach you with "My insurance ends on MM/DD/YYYY, please contact me closer to that date."

If you no longer need business insurance, please stop me from wasting both of our time by continuing to try to contact you. Simply reply with "I no longer need insurance. My insurance ends on MM/DD/YYYY, please contact me closer to that date."

Again, despite multiple attempts through phone calls, emails, and texts, I haven't received a response. Please respond so I will know when to contact you. This is Billy Williams with the Williams Family Insurance and Investment Group.

You can call or text me at 682-206-3836.

You can email me at billy@wfig.info

When closing the sale.

The Don't Wait Close.

"I can't promise you that the prices I quoted you today will still be the same in a couple of weeks. Because of what is going on with the cost of labor and materials, weather events, and the number of claims being reported, Insurance carriers are changing rates and guidelines regularly. Waiting could mean that you miss out on the coverage and rates I can guarantee today. If you like everything we agreed to today, I strongly suggest we go ahead an get this started today."

The Avoid Regret Close.

"As you know, the moment something bad happens and you don't have the right insurance, you would pay double or triple if you could go back and buy the insurance after the fact! Unfortunately, you can't so you are left coming out of pocket for $1000's. We have the best coverage and the best price that is available to you today. I don't want to see you delay this and regret that decision down the road. Do you want to pay the amount in full, or would monthly payments be better for you?"

Life Insurance Living Benefits Close.

"A portion of your life insurance premium payments is allocated towards a cash value account within the policy, which grows over time and can be accessed through withdrawals or policy loans.

The cash value accumulation within a whole life insurance policy grows on a tax-deferred basis, meaning you won't owe taxes on the gains until you withdraw them.

The sooner we start this policy, the sooner your money can start working for you. Are you ready to get started?

The Now That You Know Close.

"Life is ironic in a lot of ways. One thing that I have noticed is once we become aware of something, we tend to see that thing wherever we go.

It is like when you get ready to buy a car and you suddenly notice that brand of car everywhere you go.

Life Insurance is that same way. The longer you delay getting your life insurance in place, the more uncomfortable you will start to feel, because you will suddenly notice how many of your friends are sick, or when you hear of an accident, your mind will instantly wonder if they had life insurance.

Let's go ahead and get this policy in place today, so you don't have to deal with being mentally uncomfortable because you didn't pull the trigger on this sooner.

The Pros and Cons Close.

"Let's weigh the pros and cons of our discussion today. On one side, we have the benefits you'll gain from getting your insurance in place today and on the other side, you have whatever is stopping you from pulling the trigger on starting your insurance.

What is the main thing that is stopping you? If I can eliminate or reduce that issue and get you the insurance you need at a price that works for you, can we wrap this up today?

The Value Equation Close.

"The true value of a product is the features, plus the benefits, plus how it protects your quality of life, plus price.

I want to make sure we address each piece of the equation.

The commercial package we are putting in place today is going to cover the value of your building and business property, liability claims you could face, commercial auto incidents and accidents, workers comp claims, as well as giving you a commercial umbrella policy which gives you an extra million dollars on top of the one million dollars per incident and up to 3 million dollars total coverage.

If we add up how much total coverage the insurance company is on the hook for it could be well over $10 Million Dollars in a worst-case scenario.

But instead of you having to come up with $10 Million Dollars, we will transfer the risk to the insurance company for $20,000 a year.

That is 0.2 or 2% of what you would have to come up with without the proper insurance in place. That transfer of risk protects your cash flow, your assets, and your overall quality of life.

Do you want to take care of this in one payment, or do you want to spread it out over the year?"

CHAPTER 6 Tools that will help you to maximize your best responses:

Pocket-Guide Scripts and Templates Download Folder

(Save the time and energy of trying to copy and retype the tons of templates provided in the pocket-guide by ordering the "Pocket-Guide Best Responses Scripts and Templates Download Folder!" See www.salesobjectionspocketguide.com for details.)

Data Super Center Customer Relationship Management Tool (CRM).

There are many awesome CRM tools available to a business today, but there is only one that contains all of the merge field ready, scripts and templates provided in the Sales Objection Pocket-Guide, as well as prewritten automated workflows that put all of the phone scripts, email templates, text message templates, and video emails into the proper send schedules with one or two clicks of a button! See https://www.inspireanation.org/Data-Super-Center for details.)

Pictory.ai Video Creation Tool

Like CRM's, you have a slew of video creation tools to choose from, but we still recommend you go with the industry standards of Zoom and Loom, as well as Pictory.ai to easily create professional videos. Here is a discount code that you can use for pictory.ai: https://pictory.ai/?ref=billy16

Calendly Appointment Scheduling Tool

Again, a wide selection of appointment scheduling tools are available to you, but we use and recommend Calendly.

Insurance Agent Coaching and Mentoring with Inspire a Nation Business Mentoring Svc.

https://www.inspireanation.org/membershipinformation

The Inspire a Nation Business Mentoring Insurance Agent Coaching and Mentoring Program will not only give you all the scripts and templates located in the Sales Objection Pocket-Guide, but our mentoring program will change the culture and trajectory of your insurance agency by providing:

- Weekly, bi-weekly, or monthly one-on-one mentoring, coaching, and role-play sessions with Dr. Williams or one of his expert mentors,

- Step-by-step procedure manuals and processes that make it almost paint-by-the-numbers simple to implement processes in your agency,

- Video training that makes it easy for you to duplicate the process,

- Screen capture pdfs that are easy to follow,

- Easy to use tasks checklist that break the tasks into a simple list,

- Phone Scripts, email, text message, and social networking templates,

- Video scripts that can be used for marketing or personalized video outreach,

- Fillable forms, Merge field ready documents,

- Complete process and training manuals,

- Best practice marketing campaigns,

- Live role-play sessions, and

- Much, much, more

I want to thank you for using this pocket-guide to help you grow your business!

Please share the link to the pocket-guide with your friends, family members, co-workers, and peers that can benefit from the information contained in this Sales Objections Pocket-Guide.

Here is a shareable link:
https://www.amazon.com/dp/B0CKQ2QWVM

Billy R. Williams, Ph.D.

President

Williams Family Insurance and Investment Group (www.wfig.info)

And Inspire a Nation Business Mentoring Svc.
(www.inspireanation.org)

www.ingramcontent.com/pod-product-compliance
Lightning Source LLC
Chambersburg PA
CBHW062351290526
45794CB00005B/2176